“CREDIT IS FOR POOR PEOPLE”

Corey P Smith

Editor: Corey P Smith

www.coreypsmith.com

Cover Design: Felix Walker

Book Design: Essex Graphix

ISBN: 9780976720843

Library of Congress Catalog Card Number: On File

Library of Congress Control Number: On File

Printed in the United States of America

The Credo Company LLC

3238 Players Club Circle

Memphis, TN 38125

www.coreypsmith.com

DISCLAIMER

This publication is designed to provide accurate and authoritative information with regard to the subject matter covered. While all of the stories described in the book are based on true experiences, most of the names are pseudonyms, and some situations have been changed slightly for educational purposes and to protect each individuals privacy. It is sold with the understanding that the publisher is not engaged in rendering legal or other professional advice. If legal advice or other expert assistance is required, the services of a competent professional person should be sought.

The authors and publisher specifically disclaim all responsibility for any liability, loss, or risk, personal or otherwise, which is incurred as a consequence, directly or indirectly, of the use and application of any of the contents of this book. The Credo Company, its Logo and Marks are trademarks of The Credo Company LLC.

Contents

Authors Statement

I would like to tell you a story that I once heard. It was about a homeless guy. There was a guy who seen a homeless man at Popeyes in Memphis and he gave him some loose dollar bills from his pocket. The homeless man said, "thank you" and so the guy asked him, "How did you get to this point?" He looked up, smiled and said, "Showing Love." The guy responded by saying, "What do you mean?" The homeless guy responded by saying, "I went through my whole life making sure everyone else was ok, no matter what was going right or wrong in my life, I did for others. I never wanted to see others go without." The guy asked the homeless man, Do You Regret It?" The homeless man said No, it just hurt me to my soul that the very people I gave the shirt off my back to help, wouldn't give me a sleeve off that same shirt when I was in need. He said, "It's better to build your own house and invite someone in for shelter, than to hand them your bricks while you are building yours, because if you keep handing them bricks from the house that you are supposed to be building for yourself, you will turn around one day and that spot where you have planned to build your house will be an empty lot, then you are the one that is looking for bricks or begging for the life you once envisioned."

I shared this story because most people do not understand the spirit of survival, manipulation and control. All three of these spirits affect the hearts and souls of most human beings at some point in their lives, especially those who are able to acquire power and wealth. After that, the number one spirit that takes over is control. And who are those that have the most control? The Insurance Companies, Banks Social Media Giants and yes, the Credit Bureaus. And you want know how they do it? The trick of creating chaos and then seizing power under the pretense of putting things back in order. This is a tried and true method of deception and manipulation. It's the meaning behind the Latin motto: ORDO AB CHAO meaning ORDER OUT OF CHAOS!

Hope Is Being Able To See That There Is Light Despite All Of The Darkness

-Desmond Tutu

CHAPTER I

Born Into Poverty

When most people are born they don't know what they are being born into, meaning Poverty or Wealth. For the great majority the answer is usually POVERTY. As for me, it was Poverty. The Thing about it, like most kids I was still Happy, because I didn't actually know that I was Poor. You see the difference between being Poor and Being Rich is like a bad drug. Once you get exposed to something that gives you a high that you never experienced before you become addicted.

That was me at seven years old. I was happy living in the projects with my mother playing football, riding my bike, roller skating and eating whatever my mom coked at night. All of that begin to change once I visited my father in California. My father was not rich, but his life was quite different than the one I had been living for the past seven years. My dad was Captain in the marines stationed in San Diego, California not too far from the ocean. For a kid like me coming from Memphis, Tennessee this was rich to me, simply because it was another level that I hadn't seen before. My reason for telling you this is, because I figured this out when I was seven and many people do not figure this out until they are twenty seven or thirty seven, and by then the struggle has gotten a little bit harder and so has the dream.

I know that you are probably asking yourself, What does this have to do with credit? EVERYTHING! Let me explain something to you, most people have always felt like I was speaking about credit from a stand point of having good credit, so that you can use it when necessary. But, I was talking about credit from a completely different prospective and that prospective was not depending on credit as a need, but utilizing credit as a luxury.

Prior to 2008, I was living my life fast. I had luxury cars, took luxury vacations, and living in a luxurious home. Essentially my entire life was a life of luxury. All of that changed in May 2008. That morning, I went walking with my wife, happy and believing that my life was safe. My wife and I were gone to the park for about two hours, and when we returned home the locks on our house had been changed and all of our stuff had been placed of the sidewalk. You see, my attitude towards credit was get as much credit as you can and burn it up in the end. Including other people that had allowed me to use their credit as well. As far as my house, I had really gotten into being a sovereign citizen thinking that I could take my house from the bank simply because they could not provide a signed promissory note. Well the joke was on me in the end from credit to uniform commercial code. It was at that moment looking at my wife crying and my kids with no place to call home anymore, that was truly a game being played and I was not even in it. The rules to this game the stakes was much higher. Life was not about Uniform Commercial Code, credit or burning what you think you may not need again, because you have cash and for the next several years, I was truly going to learn the Game Of Credit.

“You Can Be Young Without Money, But You Can’t Be Old Without It”

-Tennessee Williams

CHAPTER II

The Birth Of Credit

Many people have no idea when the whole system of credit started and why it was even put in place. Remember in my book the Conspiracy of Credit I said, "Credit Is For Poor People." The reason that I said that, was because poor people will always trade time for money. This means no matter how much you work you will never make enough money to truly live a life with financial freedom. Well guess what, Time and Money really is not the true cost of financial freedom. It is Information. I am going to give you a brief history about the bullshit that they call CREDIT, because it goes deeper than even the credit bureaus.

In the 1970's America started to outsource a lot of business such as the steel and automotive industries until eventually they shut down. Many of the industrial jobs were replaced by jobs in the service industries like Walmart and McDonalds.

You see in 1978 the Supreme court prevented states from enforcing laws to cap interest rates for banks, so the banks became loan sharks. In the 1980's deregulation of banks and deindustrialization took a toll on the people that previously worked in the industrial and automotive industry in which they were paid decent wages, but due to the deregulation of banks and the outsourcing of jobs forcing them into the new emerging service industry, which paid lower wages. So they could not survive and so they had to turn to consumer credit. This caused debt to become part of the working class life. Consumer debt became a substitute for good jobs and good wages. Debt had been around, but it was used mainly to finance cars and houses. I will go into more detail about how the housing and insurance industry are two of the main catalyst for this Game of Credit.

Now think about this! Because the more people had to rely on low wages and credit, the deeper they went into debt and the banks learn to take advantage of this situation. They figured out how to target poor people who depended on debt and who truly would struggle to pay it back. Andrew Kahr, founder of Providian bank said, "It didn't require a lot of investigation to see that the people who paid their debt in full every month were not profitable." Banks called these people revolvers, because they maxed themselves out, therefore the banks could make more money off of the interest rates. Remember the deregulation of banks allowed them to charge high interest rates. And these same people were living from paycheck to paycheck. They needed Debt! The banks knew this so the credit card and lending industry expanded. So the banks collected as much information as they could on consumers and by doing this they could create Algorithms. Remember when I talked about Algorithms in my books the Conspiracy of Credit and How To Outsmart The Credit Bureaus. Well, by developing Algorithms on people who depended on credit and debt the most, they could essentially create a caste system as well. Which could easily be used to mask discrimination and determine which consumers could make them the most money.

In 1975 the first FICO was developed but, in 1989 the first general FICO score was introduced. This whole design was created to identify what was called revolvers. These are the people considered the money makers and their true customers. This is the reason why in 1995 one of the directors at Experian said, "Modeling just credit risk is passe', The real risk is that a customer is not profitable." That is the reason why they only targeted working class people who needed credit. This is why subprime lending grew as fast as it did in the 1980's, because the banks could prey on poor people. And remember when I said, "Algorithms could be used to mask discrimination." Well that is why Wells Fargo gave their loan officers incentives to target the black communities and give even the people who qualified for the better interest rates subprime loans. They called the Ghetto Loans. You see, the goal was never to help the customer, it was to make money. Credit is a tool for discipline and control. Think about this, credit scores do not reflect financial health. An example of financial health would be how you budget or how much you save. But, a credit score and report allows the bank to determine whether you are a profitable customer or not. That means how much debt do you carry from one month to the next. The American economy is unequal and preys on the poor. Remember when I told you that at some point most people will be affected by one of the three spirits, with the most dominant being the spirit of control. Well control is the cousin to slavery and the banks along with insurance companies created a product that would forever keep people in debt and manipulated people into believing that it was a dream come true. That dream and debt is called a mortgage. The word mortgage is an old French word that means “dead pledge.”

Let me take you a little deeper with this concept of buying a house. Before the whole idea of owning a house existed, almost everyone lived on land that was owned by someone else, similar to sharecropping, but not having to farm the land. The king would own the land and would give it to Lords and churches. The Lords would in turn give land to the knights and the peasants would pay rent to the knights and the clergy. Think about what I said, “the peasants would pay rent to the knights and the clergy.” The clergy being the church. Remember when I talked about the three spirits. In my book Conspiracy of Credit, I make reference to politics, religion, education and banking being connected in order to control the masses of people. I am making reference to the dark ages because I am trying to paint a picture for you to understand how this entire economic system has evolved into something that will eventually birth a world of have and have nots again.

This Dark Ages blueprint was duplicated in the United States evolving from sharecropping into the birth of the Industrial Revolution. Now keep in mind that insurance companies had been around since 1752 and becoming more powerful by the year. As the banks and insurance companies began to work together they also started to recognize the power of debt and manipulating people into it. You have to remember that both banks and insurance companies are both financial institutions. And remember in my book How To Outsmart The Credit Bureaus I explained how some of the credit bureaus started out as insurance companies. One of the biggest things that the banks realized, was that instead of people renting land they could make money off of a more tangible asset that could translate into real world money. The banks figured they could buy land for cheap, sign a contract to sell the land and provide a loan to build a house on that same land and make money off the sale as well. Remember how I explained the Dark Ages and Kings owned the land, well now the local government collects the tax payments on the land as rent instead of Lords and Knights.

All of this eventually translated into a lending system that improved with the help of deregulation, outsourcing, and the FICO score that was designed to make money off the working class with the invention of the mortgage leading all profitable debts.

“The Power To Do Good Is Also The Power To Do Harm”

-Milton Friedman

CHAPTER III

How Credit Became The Con

I once asked the question to an interviewer, "Who Is The Most Dangerous? A Con Man or Robber?" His response was a robber, but he was wrong. A Con man can do you much more harm than a robber. You see a robber comes to rob, that is what he does, that is all he knows. And his sites are only on one thing that could translate into money. Well a Con man can affect not just your life, but also the people who are connected to you. Now, think about the Con man and Robber analogy in terms of institutions such banks, insurance companies, large corporations and credit bureaus.

After so many times being broke and blocked from having the finer things in life, I started to evaluate how did I end up in this predicament again. Why was I broke and everything pointed back to a system that had many players whose sole purpose was to keep me on a treadmill of debt and I was supposed to stay there.

Our economy and financial industry is made up of debt and taxes. These two factors alone will prevent any person who is working a job from ever becoming financially free. Now divide these two factors with credit and you will forever live in poverty. So, the one thing that I want you to remember as I explain how credit became the Con is that rich people never work for money they live off passive income and their biggest expense is taxes. And one of the hardest things to tax is passive income because the rich people are really not working a job anyway. They OWN!

Lets define what a Con really means. The definition of Con is to persuade someone to do or believe something, typically by use of a deception. Well one of the first things banks, credit card companies and credit bureaus made you believe was that having good credit was the equivalent to being an astute money manager. They also convinced you to be proud of a FICO score that is only a representation of how much debt you can manage. And the government assist these institutions by governing what debt and payment information can be included and excluded in credit reports as well as how long. All of this information ultimately determines a persons credit score or should I say FICO. Now every Con has a foundation of manipulation in the first place. This has to be done in order to set the stage for the true Con. Those elements include education, religion, banking and politics. In other words, the powers that be have to get the peoples mind right. Remember when I explained the trick of creating chaos and then seizing power, well that power is seized by way of controlling the masses through credit scores.

When I said, “Credit Is For Poor People,” it is because they are controlled by the system and can be attacked whenever they get out of line. Through heir housing, by being evicted, their wages by being garnished, through their transportation, by their cars being repossessed, and sued publicly, which could pushed them into bankruptcy. And most of all they can be taxed the most because of their lack of information and money. This is the reason I said, that rich people live off of passive income and are able to hide behind the corporations that they own. This also allows them to evade high taxes and all of the things I just mentioned such as eviction, garnishment, repossession and most of all bankruptcy.

Take a look at the highway system throughout America. This system was not exactly designed by mistake or because it is some great architectural design. It had a lot to do with racial segregation and concentrated poverty. Now let's talk about how America convinced many people to take the pledge of death.

"It Takes As Much Energy To Wish As It Does To Plan"

-Eleanor Roosevelt

CHAPTER IV

How To Buy House

One of the greatest dreams for a woman is to own a house and the greatest aspirations of a man is to make that dream come true. The problem with this dream is many people do not understand this monopoly game that is truly being played with them as the pawns in the game. I explained in a previous chapter about how the entire housing market is rigged by the banks with the assistance of the government to be nothing more than a loan shark operation, that is too big too fail.

It is true that mortgages are nothing more than a product created in order to perpetuate a cycle of debt. And the cycle is perfected with the introduction of the FICO scoring system. In my book How To Outsmart The Credit Bureaus, I broke down how the credit bureaus enable the banks to create a caste system using Algorithms to mask discrimination especially when it comes to housing.

I am going to explain discrimination and redlining, it is not just based on race, but also on socioeconomic status as well. The idea of the mortgage system initially started in England and was later introduced into the United States housing market around the 1930's. Remember when I told you earlier that insurance companies, not the banks came up with the whole idea of mortgages as a way to take advantage of poor people. The reason I make reference to the mortgage system being a big loan sharking ring, is because the entire system of mortgage lending is based off interest rates and fifteen to thirty year mortgages. You see the insurance companies motivation for this system was to put poor people in financial bondage with the opportunity to take their property if they fail behind on their payments. This scheme would pay even more in the rental business.

I am going to explain something that I talked about in the previous chapter regarding Ghetto loans being made by Wells Fargo bank. You see poor people have always been an opportunity for banks to make money off of their ignorance. And the assistance of the educational system helped feed this poor mans mentality through behavioral routines, other peoples ideas and books. Essentially creating sheep. The term ghettos expanded into impoverished housing communities. You Know? THE HOOD!

The FHA underwriters warned that the presence of one or two non-whites could under mind the real estate value in the suburbs. These government guidelines were quickly adopted by the private industries, and in the 1930's the government institutionalized the national appraisal system and race played a major role in this system. The system was used to evaluate 239 cities across the country for financial risk. Keep in mind the words financial risk and algorithms being utilized in a system that was created to determine who could afford to buy a house or should I say, where they would be allowed to buy a house.

This system basically gave the all white communities that were far away from the black communities the highest rating of GREEN. Those communities that were minority communities were given the lowest rating of RED. They were REDLINED!

Two things I would like to point out, and that is rating and redlining. Even as of today this practice is still being disguised through credit score, zip codes, and mortgages. Because the minority communities were given a low rating when it came to the financial risk of mortgage approvals, this affected the property values in these communities. This means that the homes in the white communities appreciated in value. This also meant that their net worth grew because they were gaining equity in the value of their homes which enabled some of them to embark into entrepreneurship.

However, it was the exact opposite when it came to the minority communities. You see in the 1950's and sixties, when the housing market did open up to blacks and minorities it was a rental market, but guess what? You cannot gain equity from paying RENT! There is a thing called housing and wealth and most Americans hold most of their wealth in the form of home equity. This is how many of them were able to finance many business ventures as well as retirement. The minorities were not able to make these kind of moves simply because public policy had already determined that this mortgage system was created to make money off the poor and generate more wealth for the banks and insurance companies. Now keep in mind everything that you witnessing today is just a more complexed system that has evolved due to technology.

Many people believed that HUD which stands for Housing and Urban Development was meant to benefit minorities when it came to home buying, but in actuality HUD played a vital role in helping contain blacks in their own neighborhood. HUD encouraged racially restricted covenants, redlining in every major city particularly the 239 cities that were evaluated for financial risk. This is where Urban Renewal came from, simply the removal of black people. The Urban Renewal plan included a federally funded highway system, which was designed to bulldoze through black neighborhoods.

“Power Is Only Given To Those Who Are Prepared To Lower Themselves To Pick It Up”

-Ragnar Lothbrok

CHAPTER V

Social Credit

Many people have been so distracted by social media with apps such as Facebook, Instagram, Twitter (X), and Tiktok that they are the very Social Media Corporations that will usher them right into the Social Credit System. You see banks and insurance companies have unbelievable power in politics and they practice political discrimination in many ways that the American people have no idea what is going on.

Some people do not realize the technology used to track their habits and behavior to create environmental and social credit scores. This technology is mainly being introduced in the private sector, primarily through insurance companies, banks and Tech companies. Just this year at the World Economic Forum, the president of Alibaba stated, "that they were developing an individual carbon footprint tracker." He said, "We are developing through technology, an ability for consumers to measure their own carbon footprint." So basically what this individual carbon footprint tracker does is collect data about where consumers travel, what they eat, what they watch and so forth. The only thing about this, is that it is already happening.

Let us go a little bit deeper. Doconomy a climate tech startup company which is in partnership with Mastercard has developed a credit card that can track your carbon footprint purchases. This includes travel and food, and can cut off once you reach a certain limit. And for those people who do not like to carry a wallet or phone everywhere they go, a company called Walletmor has developed a chip that can be implanted in the hand and it has all of your personal information and all you have to do is just wave your hand over a sensor.

There are a few things working in the world of credit right now. One is the FICO10T and the other is ESG which stands for Environmental, Social, and Governance. This year Standard & Poors, one of the worlds top credit rating corporations announced that ESG scoring would be expanding to include American states as well. In addition to that, FICO, the consumer credit rating agency stated that personal ESG scores would soon follow. They also stated, "This would include property energy ratings data in mortgage valuation and decisioning." The ESG credit scoring can be more harmful to poor people than the FICO10T, the reason I say this, is because the FICO10T score was only going back two years which would cause a problem for the credit repair industry, but the ESG scoring would ultimately kill the credit repair industry.

Justin Haskins, director at the Heartland Institute said, "I think it is highly likely that within the next two years, you're going to see financial institutions start to use a personalized social credit score of some kind to make decisions about things like your access to loans, your interest rate, or whatever you're eligible for insurance coverage." Although I personally do not think that this will happen within the next two years, but I do believe at some point it is going to happen.

You see, the problem with all of this, is that some people think that it has to be mandated by the government in order for this to happen, but in fact it's already happening in the social media companies, banks and insurance companies. The banks, financial management companies and insurance companies will eventually be able to decide how we live. They will soon be the new legislature.

There is something called the Green New Deal in Congress right now! No Congress has not passed it yet, but that does not matter because they don't have to pass it because the big banks, insurance companies and financial management firms are the (de facto) and they are deciding how we will function in everyday life. That is the reason I say they are becoming the new legislature.

Banks are very powerful and this was apparent when in Canada the banks froze the personal accounts of people who were protesting. The banks cut them off from their own money. No banks in the United States haven't done this yet, but they have selectively denied banking and payment services to certain people and groups they believe to be politically undesirable.

Now all of this may sound like a conspiracy theory, but whether it's an epidemic, climate change, social credit or social liberties, they surrender of a persons liberties usually comes after a crisis that is presented to people as something they must accept for the greater good of society.

"Power Is of Two Kinds. One Is Obtained By The Fear Of Punishment And The Other By Acts Of Love. Power Based On Love Is A Thousand Times More Effective And Permanent Then The One Derived From Fear Of Punishment"

-Mahatma Gandhi

CHAPTER VI

In FICO We Trust

Whatever we need to survive in this life, we need credit. If we want to start a new business we need credit, because it's basically financing. Loans are the foundation for starting and growing a business. But in order to do any of this you need a credit score. The scoring system basically ranks people on a scale of 350 which is poor to 850 which is excellent. Whatever that number is will determine whether you make it in business and in your personal life.

This system is supposed to be fair and a fact-based to determine whether to approve credit or not. But the United States is controlled by economic racism that puts poor people at a disadvantage. This type of discrimination is put into data to codify discrimination. You see it's not a black and white thing anymore, it's a poor thing. Credit scores do not level the playing field, they are the gatekeepers to wealth-building.

Before the 1974 Equal Credit Opportunity Act (ECOA), white male bankers had total control over loan approval and credit. They regularly denied black people based on their race. The passage of the Equal Credit Opportunity Act made banks use credit history and not any part of the persons identity to determine whether they got approved or not. In 1989 the three major credit bureaus started using a formula created in 1959 by two white men, that's known today as FICO.

In 1956 Earl Issac an electrical engineer joined William Fair to start up a management consultant company as a 50/50 partnership. By 1958 they introduced the first scoring system called Credit Applications Scoring Algorithms. This system was designed to predict the payment behavior of consumers including whether they would pay on time, late or not at all. Now I want you to think about that last word, ALGORITHMS.

The last 40 years in America, Fair Isaac Company has controlled our lives in some shape, form, or fashion. They were able to do this by stealing a math formula from the 9th century and called it a FICO score.

The credit and banking industry have used an Ancient Muslim mathematical formula to hijack our entire economy. The creator of the Fair Isaac Company used an algorithm created by a man named Mohammed Bin Al-Khwarizimi. Over the years they were able to perfect this predictive analytical formula.

The formula that Al-Khwarizimi created is shown below.

X={q+[q2+(r-p2)3]1/2}1/3+{q2+(r-p2)3]1/2}1/3+p

Where p=-b/(3a),q=p3+(bc3ad)/(6a2),r=c/(3a)

On top of the formula they used what is called the "Church-Turing Lambda Machine Thesis and this is how they came up with the scores. The word algorithm comes from a Muslim mathematician named Abu Abdullah Muhammad ibn Musa Al-Khwarizmi.

The word algorithm originally stands for rules of performing arithmetic using Hindu-Arabic numbers. It later evolved into European Latin translation of Al-Khwarizmi's name into algorithm by the 18th century.

I want you to think about something called Linear Regression when you think about your FICO score. Linear

Regression is a method of organizing data by using a straight line through points on a graph. This is what stock traders use everyday to predict the way the stock will go later in the day.

It's not that we don't understand some basic FICO equation information already. The problem is that your FICO score has too many variables, too many scoring models and too many moving parts, which helps them disguise the economic discrimination that takes place everyday.

“The Biggest Risk In Not Taking Any Risk. In A World That’s Changing Really Quickly, The Only Strategy That Is Guaranteed To Fail Is Not Taking Risk”

-Mark Zuckerberg

CHAPTER VII

Cracking The Code

Many people do not understand that the world is moving so fast with technology, social media and not to mention artificial intelligence software that gaining knowledge is temporary. Now you are probably wandering, what does knowledge is temporary mean. Well, remember I have always told you that knowledge is only powerful when it remains a secret because once it is exposed to the masses it becomes diluted. Well in this day and age information, which is knowledge is dispense so fast by way of the internet that the world just digest and shits it out at the speed of light, and most people do not have time to capitalize off the information.

When it comes to credit there is still a few things that the world, or should I say consumers have not figured out and that is how artificial intelligence is being used against them. Because most people are like sheep and they follow the herd. Therefore it becomes easy to manipulate them as well as expose anything that is done in similar fashion. Over the past six or seven years when it comes to credit repair almost everybody have become nothing more than parrots and only repeating what they hear other people say, and going in the same direction as the herd.

I am going to explain a way for you to use the credit bureaus own software against them and increase your chances of removing negative items from your credit report.

First you must understand that there are two pieces of software that the credit bureaus are working with, the first is called OCR which stands for Optical Character Recognition. It is used to help different institutions like banks, insurance companies and credit bureaus digitize vast amounts of paper documents such as disputes letters into different phrases or simple one to two words.

You may have been thinking that humans read your dispute letters, but you are wrong. Whenever you send a dispute letter into the credit bureaus it goes through an initial screening process and this is done by the OCR (Optical Character Recognition) program. The OCR programs scans each dispute letter thoroughly to pull out any information or keywords that it deems important or frivolous because it has seen it before. That is why after each dispute letter is scanned by OCR, it is marked as either frivolous or legitimate. Now depending on how the dispute letter is marked will determine whether or not it moves on to the next phase, which is the E-Oscar system.

Just in case you do not know what E-Oscar is, I will explain it to you. E-Oscar stands for "Online Solution For Complete And Accurate Reporting." The three credit bureaus Experian, Equifax, and Transunion created this software in1963.

Now that you know what the E-Oscar system is used for at this point, if your dispute letter makes it past the OCR program, it must still get past the E-Oscar system. Similar to the OCR program, E-Oscar also uses technology to scan your dispute letters. After each letter is scanned by the E-Oscar system it receives a two-letter code that categorizes the dispute. Your dispute will only be given validity based on the code given by the E-Oscar system. The problem with this is the technology is also communicating with so many other data friendly databases that you do not stand a chance at having certain items deleted. This is why I told you that many people have made it even more difficult by doing the same thing.

Let's talk about getting around these two systems. First of all I want you to look at the E-Oscar list of codes below because these are the codes that you want to put in any dispute letter that you create, but remember be original and do not use templates that people are selling on the internet or that credit repair companies are using.

E-OSCAR CODES	
001	Not his/hers.
002	Belongs to another individual with same/ similar name.
006	Not aware of collection.
008	Late due to change of address and never received statement.
010	Settlement or partial payments accepted.
012	Claims paid the original creditor before collection status or paid before charge-off.
014	Claims paid before collection status.
019	Included in the bankruptcy of another person.
023	Claims account closed.
024	Claims account closed by consumer.
031	Contract canceled or rescinded.

037	Account included in bankruptcy.
038	Claims active military duty.
039	Insurance claim delayed.
040	Account involved in litigation.
041	Claims victim of natural or declared disaster.
100	Claims account deferred.
101	Not liable for account (i.e. account belongs to ex-spouse, business, etc)
102	Account reaffirmed or not included in bankruptcy.
103	Claims true identity fraud/account fraudulently opened.
104	Claims account take-over, fraudulent charges made on account.
105	Disputes Dates of Last Payment/Opened/ of First Delinquency/Billing/Closed.
106	Disputes present/previous Account Status/Payment History Profile/Payment Rating.
107	Disputes Special Comment/Compliance Condition Code/narrative remarks.
108	Disputes Account Type or Terms Duration/Terms Frequency or Portfolio Type disputed.
109	Dispute current balance.
110	Claims company will change.
111	Claims company will delete.
112	Claims inaccurate information.

The one thing that you must remember, it does not matter if you send a highly detailed dispute letter with documentation, it will still be reduced to one of the twenty-six two digit codes listed in E-Oscar. So at this point you want to write very short and to the point letters with one of the two-digit codes from E-Oscar. I have provided an example of how you should structure your dispute letter.

Name
Address
DOB/SSN
Date

Credit Bureaus Address

Please remove/update the following inaccuracies found on my credit report.

[account 1] remove due to inaccuracy in dates of last payments: [date] (105)

[account 2] update for inaccurate information in the [element] [facts] (112)

[account 3] remove because account included in bankruptcy (037)

[account 4] stop reporting this account due to true identity fraud (103)

[account 5] remove authorized user because I am not liable for account (101)

Send me a new credit report reflecting these changes.

I have also provided the legal department address for all three of the major credit bureaus. You may want to send the same letters to them via certified mail.

TransUnion LLC
Attention: Office of General Counsel
555 W. Adams St.
Chicago, IL. 60661

Experian
General Counsel
475 Anton Blvd.
Costa Mesa, CA. 92626

Equifax
General Counsel
1550 Peachtree Street, NW
Atlanta, Georgia 30309

Equifax
Attention: Custodian of Records
P.O. Box 105139
Atlanta, Georgia 30348-5139

"Play By The Rules, But Be Ferocious"

-Phil Knight

CHAPTER VIII

The Invisible House

I have told you the history of how mortgages came about, but I want to tell you another story about an invisible house. The housing market has changed since 2008 and trying to buy a house since the Pandemic has gotten a whole lot harder.

The story that I am about to tell you is about a guy who bought a house with no money. You see he figured since the house was going to be the biggest debt that he would ever take on, then it should be the biggest money maker as well.

This guy planned ahead for a little over two years. One of the first things he did was establish a corporation in the state where he lived. Afterwards he established a business address, phone number, bank account and made sure that the company could easily be found on the internet. He then went back to the bank where he had opened the business checking account and applied for a merchant account. The man knew that this process would take at least two years and so he obtained as many credit cards as possible and before he knew it, after about a year, he had more than $175,000 in personal and business credit.

During this time the man would make small purchases from his merchant account by using friends, family members and his wife's credit cards and afterwards giving them their money back while eating the small cost of fee's. Around the twenty third month the man began looking for a house and after four months of searching he found the perfect home. The man than began getting all of the necessary paperwork to buy the home as well as his 5% down, because remember a conventional loan is always better than FHA, because you are not stuck with mortgage insurance for the life of the loan.

He would need tax returns and after carefully talking to his accountant and loan officer, he knew exactly how much he would have to pay the IRS. One clever thing the man did was file the taxes he needed to buy the house and immediately setup a payment plan with the IRS. The man knew all the time that he would eventually file an amendment.

Remember I told you that the man had a merchant account and also about $175,000 in personal and business credit cards. Well, this is how he put down the 5% on the house. What he did was use the credit cards that he had to make online purchases and manually credit card purchases. The reason he did this was because he could come back and dispute every charge and get his money back because the credit card was never present. I know many people might think this is shady, but every credit card has zero liability insurance up to a million dollars. So nobody lost here.

The man had everything in place that he needed to buy the house, taxes, credit, money in the bank and his down payment. So during the twenty sixth month, the man closed on the home. He got all his money back from the credit cards and eventually did an amendment on his tax returns for a lesser amount and did not have to pay the IRS as much money back.

Now that the man was successful with the purchase of the home, he immediately put the home on websites like Airbnb, Vrbo, Booking.com, Vacasa and Flipkey. The man never spent one night in the home, but eventually realized he had made over $200,000 on a house that he never called home. Although this story may sound shady and conning to some, remember the man at the beginning of the book who was homeless. You must never forget, the world will step right over you as you lie homeless, broke and hungry on the street.

“If You Can Not Explain It Simply, You Do Not Understand It Well Enough”

-Albert Einstein

CHAPTER IX

Never Too Late

There are many things that can and will hurt you in life, but none more than procrastination and being late. One of the worse things that could happen to you when you're trying to maintain a good credit score is being late on a bill. It will devastate your credit score. Many people do not believe the myth that banks and credit bureaus want you to have bad credit. You see the credit bureaus can sell your information for a higher price when you have subprime credit and the banks in turn can charge you higher interest rates because of your bad credit or even one late payment.

It is funny because some banks will still overlook your late payments, if it benefits them and their pockets. Let me tell you a little story about one bank that did not care how late some of it's customers were on their payments.

On September 28, 2003, William J. Burnell, Robert B. Calloway and Frank J. Adolph were charged with bank fraud, and what was the fraud? Late Payments. The three men ran a fraudulent scheme that led to the collapse of First NBC Bank. You see from 2006 to 2017, William J. Burnell was the bank's Chief Credit Officers. He was responsible for the bank's lending, credit, bank loans and recovery, collections and most of all the bank's past due loans. Nevertheless, Burnell conspired with bank President Ashton J. Ryan, Jr. and others to conceal past due loans so new loans could be issued to them and hiding their past due status from the Board. This is just one example of how banks can do what they want especially if, they do not get caught. The only problem here was that First NBC Bank was a small bank.

These three guys choose to try and help some customers who had late payments while helping themselves in the process, but what about the Big Banks that choose to hurt it's customers or should I say consumers.

Let me explain something about late payments, first of all everyone has more than one credit score. In fact, you have many credit scores. You may think that one late payment won't hurt you, but in reality that one payment is the single most important factors in the FICO formula.

Some people think that payments must be at least 30 days late before they affect a FICO score. The fact of the matter is, a creditor can report a payment that is even one day late. In practice they do not. As a generalization, late payments on revolving accounts do not get reported until they are 30 days late. But keep in mind these are not the rules. Now let me explain to you how to remove a late payment.

The first thing that you must remember when disputing a late payment is never do a good will letter or dispute directly with the creditor. The reason you do not want to do this is because the creditor has the true records and most people now a days pay from their own personal banking account. When you write a good will letter you are admitting guilt and you have just contacted the original creditor who has all the records and payment history it needs to prove that you were in fact late.

What you want to do is dispute with the credit bureaus and put the burden of proof back on the data furnisher and credit bureaus. Remember this could be very difficult for them because they reduce every dispute to a code from E-Oscar, make them work! I have provided three sample letters that you can use to remove late payments.

Letter One

Date
Your Name
Your Address

Credit Bureaus Name
Credit Bureaus Address
Re: Late Payment Inaccurately Reported

I have pulled my credit report both on your website as well as myfico.com and have found some inaccurate information that requires removal. I have a new employment opportunity coming up and I know they will pull my credit report, and the false information will hurt my chances of being hired.

[Capital One: account number] I was not late on April 12, 2023, which is reported as 30 days late on my [credit bureaus name], On April 17, 2023, it shows me as being 30 days on [credit bureaus name], and on April 13, 2023, it shows me as 60 days late on [credit bureaus name]. Remove this late payment for inaccuracy and update to paid as agreed.

Thank You
[Your Name]

Letter Two

Date
Your Name
Your Address

Credit Bureaus Name
Credit Bureaus Address
Re: Late Payment Inaccurately Reported

I have pulled my credit report both on your website as well as myfico.com and have found some inaccurate information that requires removal. I have a new employment opportunity coming up and I know they will pull my credit report, and the false information will hurt my chances of being hired.

[Capital One: account number] This late payment on June 10, 2023 requires removal because I paid on time. Please furnish the bank statement belonging to Capital One Bank, proving that I was ever late on this account. If you cannot furnish this bank statement (which is the only legal form of verification), this account must be updated to paid on time never late for false reporting.

Thank You
[Your Name]

Letter Three

Date
Your Name
Your Address

Credit Bureaus Name
Credit Bureaus Address
Re: Late Payment Inaccurately Reported

I have pulled my credit report both on your website as well as myfico.com and have found some inaccurate information that requires removal. I have a new employment opportunity coming up and I know they will pull my credit report, and the false information will hurt my chances of being hired.

[Capital One: account number] Update to paid as agreed I was not late.

Thank You
[Your Name]

One other method that is highly effective if all else fails is to mail a certified dispute letter to the CEO's office of the three major credit bureaus. What you want to do is get the letter notarized, send it overnight and request signature addressed to the CEO. Include your phone number, email address and make sure that the letter is original and not from a template. You also want to attach a copy of (15 USC 6802B) to your letter as well. The reason all of this is so important and you want to disputed through the credit bureaus is because of the privacy laws. The Act (Title VI of the Consumer Credit Protection Act) protects information collected by consumer reporting agencies such as credit bureaus, medical information companies and tenant screening services. Information in a consumer report cannot be provided to anyone who does not have a purpose specified in the ACT! I have provided the address and email to each CEO of the three major credit bureaus and a copy of (15 USC 6802 B)

§6802. Obligations with respect to disclosures of personal information

(a) Notice requirements

Except as otherwise provided in this subchapter, a financial institution may not, directly or through any affiliate, disclose to a nonaffiliated third party any nonpublic personal information, unless such financial institution provides or has provided to the consumer a notice that complies with section 6803 of this title.

(b) Opt out

(1) In general

A financial institution may not disclose non-public personal information to a nonaffiliated third party unless-

(A) such financial institution clearly and conspicuously discloses to the consumer, in writing or in electronic form or other form permitted by the regulations prescribed under section 6804 of this title, that such information may be disclosed to such third party;

(B) the consumer is given the opportunity, before the time that such information is initially disclosed, to direct that such information not be disclosed to such third party; and

(C) the consumer is given an explanation of how the consumer can exercise that nondisclosure option.

(2) Exception

This subsection shall not prevent a financial institution from providing nonpublic personal information to a nonaffiliated third party to perform services for or functions on behalf of the financial institution, including marketing of the financial institution's own products or services, or financial products or services offered pursuant to joint agreements between two or more financial institutions that comply with the requirements imposed by the regulations prescribed under section 6804 of this title, if the financial institution fully discloses the providing of such information and enters into a contractual agreement with the third party that requires the third party to maintain the confidentiality of such information.

(c) Limits on reuse of information

Except as otherwise provided in this subchapter, a nonaffiliated third party that receives from a financial institution nonpublic personal information under this section shall not, directly or through an affiliate of such receiving third party, disclose such information to any other person that is a nonaffiliated third party of both the financial institution and such receiving third party, unless such disclosure would be lawful if made directly to such other person by the financial institution.

(d) Limitations on the sharing of account number information for marketing purposes

A financial institution shall not disclose, other than to a consumer reporting agency, an account number or similar form of access number or access code for a credit card account, deposit account, or transaction account of a consumer to any nonaffiliated third party for use in telemarketing, direct mail marketing, or other marketing through electronic mail to the consumer.

(e) General exceptions

Subsections (a) and (b) shall not prohibit the disclosure of nonpublic personal information-

(1) as necessary to effect, administer, or enforce a transaction requested or authorized by the consumer, or in connection with-

(A) servicing or processing a financial product or service requested or authorized by the consumer;

(B) maintaining or servicing the consumer's account with the financial institution, or with another entity as part of a private label credit card program or other extension of credit on behalf of such entity; or

(C) a proposed or actual securitization, secondary market sale (including sales of servicing rights), or similar transaction related to a transaction of the consumer;

(2) with the consent or at the direction of the consumer;

(3) (A) to protect the confidentiality or security of the financial institution's records pertaining to the consumer, the service or product, or the transaction

therein; (B) to protect against or prevent actual or potential fraud, unauthorized transactions, claims, or other liability; (C) for required institutional risk control, or for resolving customer disputes or inquiries; (D) to persons holding a legal or beneficial interest relating to the consumer; or (E) to persons acting in a fiduciary or representative capacity on behalf of the consumer;

(4) to provide information to insurance rate advisory organizations, guaranty funds or agencies, applicable rating agencies of the financial institution, persons assessing the institution's compliance with industry standards, and the institution's attorneys, accountants, and auditors;

(5) to the extent specifically permitted or required under other provisions of law and in accordance with the Right to Financial Privacy Act of 1978 [12 U.S.C. 3401 et seq.], to law enforcement agencies (including the Bureau of Consumer Financial Protection [1] a Federal functional regulator, the Secretary of the Treasury with respect to subchapter II of chapter 53 of title 31, and chapter 2 of title I of Public Law 91–508 (12 U.S.C.

1951–1959), a State insurance authority, or the Federal Trade Commission), self-regulatory organizations, or for an investigation on a matter related to public safety;

(6) (A) to a consumer reporting agency in accordance with the Fair Credit Reporting Act [15 U.S.C. 1681 et seq.], or (B) from a consumer report reported by a consumer reporting agency;

(7) in connection with a proposed or actual sale, merger, transfer, or exchange of all or a portion of a business or operating unit if the disclosure of nonpublic personal information concerns solely consumers of such business or unit; or

(8) to comply with Federal, State, or local laws, rules, and other applicable legal requirements; to comply with a properly authorized civil, criminal, or regulatory investigation or subpoena or summons by Federal, State, or local authorities; or to respond to judicial process or government regulatory authorities having jurisdiction over the financial institution for examination, compliance, or other purposes as authorized by law.

(Pub. L. 106–102, title V, §502, Nov. 12, 1999, 113 Stat. 1437 ; Pub. L. 111–203, title X, §1093(2), July 21, 2010, 124 Stat. 2095.)

Equifax
Mark W. Begor
1550 Peachtree Street NW
Atlanta, Georgia 30309-2402
Mark.begor@equifax.com
404-885-8000

Brian Cassin
Experian Corporate Headquarters
475 Anton Blvd.
Costa Mesa, CA. 92626
Brian.cassin@experianplc.com
714-830-7000

TransUnion
Christoper A. Cartwright
555 W. Adams St.
Chicago, IL. 60661-3614
ccartwright@transunion.com
312-985-2000

"Every Problem Is A Gift-Without Problems We Would Not Grow"

-Anthony Robbins

CHAPTER X

The Bankrupt Millioniare

There are many poor people that believe bankruptcy was designed for when you are broke and have nothing left. In fact, it is the exact opposite. It was designed as a way for the wealthy to keep their money and assets.

Donald Trump is worth about three billion dollars, but how can a man who has filed bankruptcy so many times, but yet still be so rich. The first thing you have to understand is that it was never personal. He filed for corporate bankruptcy four times, in 1991, 1992,2004 and 2009. He has never filed for personal bankruptcy and the ability to still remain financially unscath.

In 1991, the first time he filed for bankruptcy was the one time his personal fortune was at risk. But, he learned from it and he insulated. More importantly, he stop guaranteeing debt with his own money.

Donald Trump began to understand that bankruptcy was a business tool. A business tool that is used by great entrepreneurs to restructure debt and free up money, while improving their business at the same time. Trump even once said, "I've used the laws of the country to my advantage and to other people's advantage."

You see most people think bankruptcy and think of losing their home, car, and money. Donald Trump understood that bankruptcy was not for houses, cars, and money. It was for business and financial success masked as failure. For most people true enough, it is about losing the cars and houses, but for the rich it's not. Most poor people only understand chapter 7 and chapter 13 bankruptcy. The rich understand the distinction between different types of bankruptcies.

For rich people and celebrities, they never file for personal bankruptcy. You as an entity and a business entity are separate things, in a legal sense. Business finances are ringfenced from your personal finances. This is why you always want to keep it business to guard your own personal assets against failure.

The word "broke" to the average person usually means empty bank accounts, refrigerators and empty pockets.

Bankruptcy is all about the chapters, chapter 7, chapter 13, and chapter 11. You see chapter 11 bankruptcy only accounted for 7,234 of 936,795 filings in the United States last year. Rich people who are often corporations unto themselves can always take advantage of a Chapter 11 bankruptcy. This is one of the differences between the rich and poor. Rich people are always thinking business and poor people are always thinking personal. It's Never Personal!

Think about this, the United States Bankruptcy Codes were drafted in the 1970's, just like the Fair Credit Reporting Act. I only explained how bankruptcy benefit the rich more than the poor, because I wanted you to truly understand the difference between personal and business. The Point Is, Think Business.

Now for those of you who have made the mistake of filing Chapter 7 or Chapter 13 bankruptcy, let me explain a way for you to remove it from your personal credit.

Remember in my first book "How To Outsmart The Credit Bureaus" how I explained how one man used the cut and paste method to remove a bankruptcy from his credit. This tactic still works, but there is something else you can do in addition to the cut and paste method.

After you have completed the cut and paste method, you also need to file a complaint against the bankruptcy court. You will need to contact the U.S. Trustee Program field office. A list of Program field offices can be found at Nationwide Office Locator. You will be asked to make a written complaint. This complaint should be very vague and simple because you only want a response from them to attach to the bankruptcy petition. Your written complaint can read "The bankruptcy trustee is reporting debt to the credit bureaus that I am not responsible for at this time." Once they respond to you, attach a copy of that letter to your dispute with the credit bureaus.

Remember credit bureaus can only verify bankruptcies by name and address only. You see Pursuant to Rule 1005 of the Federal Rules of Bankruptcy Procedure, all documents filed with the court are to contain only the last four digits of the individuals social security number or tax-identification number. If you file a bankruptcy Pro Se the rules allow you to file a motion to seal documents.

This means the only information released to third parties who are not involved directly with your case is (1) full name, (2) the last four digits of the social security number and (3) your address. This is also why it is important to remove multiple addresses from your credit report. It does not help the credit bureaus, that the Federal bankruptcy courts in no way report to the credit bureaus, nor do they act in conjunction with any consumer reporting agencies. I have provided a short letter that you can use when writing the bankruptcy court.

Corey P Smith
1234 Credit Road
Atlanta, Ga. 30348

Clerk of Court
Address
City, State

To Whom It May Concern,

My name is Corey P. Smith, and I am writing you because an entry appears on my credit report which states that I filed bankruptcy in your district. Could you please explain to me how this might have occurred? From my understanding only the last four digits of a debtors social security number are released to third parties, pursuant to the Federal Rules of Bankruptcy Procedure. Any information you can provide me with would be greatly appreciated.

Sincerely,
Corey P Smith

"Without Passion You Don't Have Energy, Without Energy You Have Nothing"

-Donald Trump

CHAPTER XI

Poverty On Repeat

Why is Credit For Poor People? The bible says, money answers all things, but poor people have no money, they only have their name and they are born into that name. A name is the first gift given to you when you are born.

Poverty is a cycle that starts when a child is born into a poor family. Their families usually have no access to resources that could help them advance in life, and usually they are trap in poverty.

On January 4, 1975 Gerald Ford, signed into law HR 17045 of the Health and Human Services, which gave birth to the Child Support Enforcement (CSE) program. It is a program that is supposed to strengthen families by collecting money for children from their noncustodial parent. But, was it really for the children. All I can think about is when children were forced to go to public schools because the government wanted women to go to work, so that they could collect taxes from women. So it was not all about children going to school. I just always question the government when they do something for the sake of the children.

Think about this, God is the creator of life. Which means he already made provisions for man, woman and child to survive no matter what, place to live, food to eat, and water to drink. He essentially planned for the creation of family. The problem is with all the technology, social media, banks, credit bureaus, politics, and entertainment destroying families has become very profitable.

How is it that a man and woman can get together and create a child or children with no interference from the law or politics being involved, but just as with marriage and divorce, Child Support has become very profitable for the United States. I want to talk about child support because not only has it become a financial weight to many men, it also destroys their credit and they cannot figure out how to resolve it. There is a reason child support not only affect your drivers license, passport, banking account and most of all your credit. Child support is not a loan or a revolving line of credit, but it is a contract that should not be reported to a credit bureau.

Can you remove child support from your credit report? The answer is Yes! I want you to look at this statue regarding child support and we will see what the Supreme Court says about child support which is a federal law, not state.

42 U.S.C. Section 666

(7) Reporting Arrearages to Credit Bureaus-

(A) In general-Procedures (subject to safeguards pursuant to subparagraph (B) requiring the state to report periodically to consumer reporting agencies (as define in section 1681 a(f) of title (15) the name of any noncustodial parent who is delinquent in the payment of support, and the amount of overdue support owed by such parent.

(B) Safeguards-Procedures ensuring that, in carrying out subparagraph (A) information with respect to a noncustodial parent is reported-

(i) only after such parent has been afforded all due process required under State law, including notice and a reasonable opportunity to contest the accuracy of such information; and

(ii) only to an entity that has furnished evidence satisfactory to the State that the entity is a consumer reporting agency (as so defined)

Now out of this statue what stands out to me the most is section (i), because every parent is afforded due process. The Child Support agencies do not verify any information, but this section affords any person due process.

Now lets look at what the statue is that defines due process within the credit bureaus.

15 U.S. Code 1681 (A)

(j) Definitions Relating to Child Support Obligations-

(i) Overdue support-

The term "overdue support" has the meaning given to such term in section 666(e) of title 42.

(2) State or local child support enforcement agency.-

The term "State or local child support enforcement agency" means a state or local agency which administers a state or local program for establishing and enforcing child support obligation.

Basically what they are saying here is, that even though Child Support is Federal program, they use state guidelines for reporting to the credit bureaus. Now lets look at the statue that defines what a "debtor" or "garnishee" means.

28 U.S. Code 3002

Definitions:

(4) "Debtor" means a person who is liable for a debt or against whom there is a claim for a debt.

(7) "Garnishee" means a person (other than the debtor) who his, or is reasonably thought to have, possession, custody, or control of any property in which the debtor has a substantial nonexempt interest, including any obligation due the debtor or to become due the debtor, and against whom a garnishment under section 3104 or 3205 is issued by a court.

All of these are regulations and codes that are contradicting what the Supreme Court says about Child Support, which is a Federal program. The Supreme Court states, "Child Support agreements are equivalent to interstate contracts and rejecting the idea that child support payment obligations are somehow 'different') (citing U.S. v. Sage, 92 F.3d at 106)." United States Court of Appeals, Second Circuit. New York.

The Supreme Court is basically telling you that Child Support is a contract. I have provided a letter for you to use in order to dispute any Child Support that may be on your credit report. But, first read this important notice that came from TransUnion.

Important Notice

Credit Reports for collection of delinquent child support, judgments, fines and liens may no longer be permitted Federal courts recently have issued rulings about the use of consumer reports for the collection of an account under the Fair Credit Reporting Act (FCRA). 1

These cases note that certain definitions were added to the FCRA as part of the 2003 amendments (FACT Act). In particular, the word "credit" was defined. As a result of the new definition the position that is being advocated is that a "collection of an account" is a permissible purpose to obtain a consumer report only when the collection is in connection with a credit transaction.

The courts have specifically rejected prior case law and FTC guidance that a judgment creditor had permissible purpose, noting that those decisions pre-dated the FACT Act. These cases have held that a delinquent child support obligation, municipal fines arising from parking tickets, and a statutory debt resulting from the towing and impound of an illegally parked vehicle did not arise from a "credit transaction." As a result, the courts found that collection of those accounts was not a valid permissible purpose to obtain a consumer report.

If you use TransUnion consumer report services in connection with the collection of an account, we advise you to promptly review the new case law with your regular attorney or compliance advisor.

TransUnion will be contacting each customer that is a third-party collector to discuss this issue. We expect to confirm with you that you are in compliance with this new interpretation. Until then, unless you advise otherwise, we are relying upon you to comply with your contract with TransUnion and this new interpretation of the law. This means that you may obtain TransUnion reports for collection purposes only when collecting on an obligation arising from a credit transaction, or where you have the written authorization of the consumer or a court order to obtain a consumer report.

As an example, for collectors of delinquent child support debt, judgments, fines, or liens, you must have in hand:

- A court order authorizing a consumer reporting agency to provide a consumer report,
- A written authorization from the debtor to obtain a consumer report, or
- Some type of contractual agreement with the consumer that rises to the level of a credit transaction under law.

1 Kevin D. Miller v. Trans Union LLC, Experian Information systems, Inc. and Supportkids, Inc., Case 1:06-cv-02883, 2/28/2007

(N.D. Illinois); Kenneth McCready vs. Linebarger Goggan Blair & Sampson, LLP, et al., Case: 06 C 4884, 8/15/2007 (N.D. Illinois), Maria E. Pintos v. Pacific Creditors Association, Experian Information Solutions,

Dispute Letter

[Your name]

[Account Number at company, if available]

[Date of birth or other identifying information requested by company]

[Your return address]

[Date]

[Company Name]

[Company address for receipt of direct disputes]

Re: Disputing error[s] on credit report

Dear [Name of company],

I am writing to request a correction of the following information that appears on my [Equifax, Experian,

TransUnion] consumer report:

Dispute 1 [These are examples. Pick the ones that apply to your credit report.]

- Account Number or other information to identify account: [Insert account number or other information such as account holder names and past addresses. This is especially important if you have had multiple accounts with the same company.]

- Dates associated with item being disputed: [Insert the date that appears on your report. This helps ensure that the correct account is identified by the company and to identify which aspects of the report are being disputed. You can still file a dispute if you don't have this date.]
- Explanation of item being disputed: [Insert a detailed explanation of why the information is inaccurate. Choose one of the choices below if it fits, or add your own description.]

The report shows I currently owe money to your company that I have already repaid. [Give details about when you paid, and attach a copy of any proof that you have.]

The date of first delinquency on my report is not accurate. [Give details about delinquency status, including payment history.]

My student loan shows a period of delinquency when I was actually in an income-driven repayment plan. [Provide documentation, including copies of your billing statements.]

I'm the victim of identity theft and I don't recognize one or more of the accounts on my report. [You may wish to include a copy of the FTC identity theft affidavit describing the identity theft.]

Other [Describe what is wrong with the report. You may include copies of any additional supporting documentation that you have.]

Dispute 2 [Continue numbering for each disputed item on your report and include the same information]

[Include the following sentence if you are including a copy of your credit report or other supporting documentation. "I have attached a copy of my report with the accounts in question circled."]

Thank you for your assistance.

Sincerely,
[Your name]

"Procrastination Is Like A Credit Card, It's A Lot Of Fun Until You Get The Bill"

-Christopher Parker

CHAPTER XII

Automated Discrimination

Many people think that Artificial Intelligence is the one piece of technology that is going to change the world or it is changing the world as we speak. But, as the old saying go, "What You Don't Know Hurt." The true fact of the matter is, that it will hurt.

Former Google employee Blake Lemoine, said the company's A.I. model was sentient. The google employee who claimed last June his company's A.I. model could already be sentient, and he was later fired by the company.

Now, what does sentient mean? It means Artificial Intelligence can feel and have experiences just as humans can. Sentient A.I. is emotionally intelligent, conscious and can perceive the world around it and turn those perceptions into emotions. In shorty sentient A.I. thinks, feels, and perceives like a person.

I want you to think about this about this for a minute, Hollywood has been giving us signs for many years through movies such as iRobot and its latest movie the Creator, and it has never had a happy ending.

Because the book is called "Credit Is For Poor People" I am going to also tell you why A.I. will bring about an end to credit repair eventually. I have been telling you about FICO scores, OCR and E-Oscar throughout the book. You see all of these systems or software is all A.I. and as it becomes more advanced with communicating with other systems that has anything to do with a persons credit, lifestyle or finances there will be no more room for disputing things that you feel are inaccurate because these systems will make decisions simply based on the information it already has complied about you and your credit.

This will eventually widening the gap even more between the rich and poor. You see machine learning is based on past decisions recorded by financial institutions datasets, the process very often consolidates existing bias and prejudice against groups defined by race, sex, sexual orientation and credit. This is simply algorithmic discrimination.

Believe it or not, credit is the blood of our economy not cash. It's critical to economic growth and the creation of jobs. Banks and financial institutions are in the business of making money and profit is their goal. They invest the money deposited with them and most of the time it's the pennies and dimes of poor people who cannot even get a loan from the bank.

To identify discrimination by using artificial intelligence is no easy task or should I say impossible. All of these systems learn from datasets that register lenders decision based on past and stored consumer reports. I told you that Hollywood has been giving us signs through movies for years, but did you get the message. Sentient A.I. can feel and have experiences just as humans and make decisions like a human, but its rational is the man, is mans own worse enemy and in order to help solve the problem for man, is to do away with man. But, in actuality the man in this instance is the poor man and what better way to destroy him other than his credit.

The Last Ten Years To Borrow More Than $4,000,000 Dollars In Loans & Lines Of This Is A List Of Banks And Credit Unions, That I Have Used Over Credit

NRL Federal Credit Union

Celtic Bank

UNIFY Financial Credit Union

Fidelity Bank

United Nations Federal Credit Union

Thrive Credit Union

Alliance Credit Union

Excite Credit Union

Balboa Capital

VyStar Credit Union

USAA

Marcus by Goldman Sachs

Justice Federal Credit Union

Island Federal Credit Union

Best Egg

Capital One Bank

Pinnacle Bank

Hope Credit Union

Chase Bank

Bank Of America

AOD Federal Credit Union

Power Financial Credit Union

Thrivent Federal Credit Union

Chevron Federal Credit Union

Fulton Bank

Bank of New York

Northern Trust

Iddeal Bank

LoanMe, Inc

Knight Capital Funding

PenFed Credit Union

Bank of Bartlett

BB&T Trust Bank

New Coast Direct

Gulf Credit Union

5 Point Credit Union

Neches Federal Credit Union

DuGood Credit Union

Randolph Brooks Federal Credit Union

Armed Forces Bank

DM Federal Credit Union

Compass Bank

Skylight Bank

Wescom Credit Union

Clarity Bank

Frost National Bank

TD Waterhouse Online Bank

nBank.com

RBC Centura

Netbank

Marketplace Bank

Pen Air Federal Credit Union

GTE Financial

Affinity Plus Federal Credit Union

American Heritage Credit Union

Chartway Federal Credit Union

Lake Michigan Credit Union

Connexus Credit Union

Nasa Federal Credit Union

River Valley Credit Union

Desco Federal Credit Union

CME Federal Credit Union

Firelands Federal Credit Union

CSE Federal Credit Union

Century Federal Credit Union

Universal 1 Credit Union

Sharefax Credit Union

Dover-Phila Federal Credit Union

Day-Air Credit Union

Pathways Financial Credit Union

Atomic Credit Union

Homeland Credit Union

Ohio University Credit Union

Kemba Credit Union

Telhio Credit Union

Directions Credit Union

Cinfed Federal Credit Union

Sun Federal Credit Union

BMI Federal Credit Union

Wright-Patt Credit Union

General Electric Credit Union

Superior Credit Union

717 Credit Union

Kemba Financial Credit Union

St. Cloud Financial Credit Union

Anoka Hennepin Credit Union

St. Paul Federal Credit Union

First Alliance Credit Union

North Shore Federal Credit Union

Dawson Co-Op Credit Union

Great River Federal Credit Union

SouthPoint Financial Credit Union

MinnCO Credit Union

My Credit Union

TruStar Federal Credit Union

Co-Op Credit Union of Montevideo Credit

SharePoint Credit Union

St. Cloud Financial Credit Union

Mayo Employees Credit Union

City & County Credit Union

Members Cooperative Credit Union

Ideal Credit Union

TopLine Federal Credit Union

Mid Minnesota Federal Credit Union

Wings Financial Credit Union

TruStone Financial Credit Union

Affinity Plus Federal Credit Union

SPIRE Credit Union

Hiway Credit Union

Central Minnesota Union

RTP Federal Credit Union

NOVA Credit Union

WNC Community Credit Union

Welcome Credit Union

Bragg Mutual Federal Credit Union

Telco Community Credit Union

Mountain Credit Union

First Flight Federal Credit Union

Duke Federal Credit Union

Carolinas Telco Federal Credit Union

Fort Bragg Federal Credit Union

Piedmont Advantage Credit Union

Members Credit Union

Champion Credit Union

Summit Credit Union

Self-Help Credit Union

Charlotte Metro Credit Union

Marine Federal Credit Union

Latino Community Credit Union

State Employees Credit Union

Coastal Federal Credit Union

Truliant Federal Credit Union

Local Government Federal Credit Union

Allegacy Federal Credit Union

Truity Credit Union

United Federal Credit Union

Altra Federal Credit Union

Red River Credit Union

Fort Smith Teachers Federal Credit Union

Patterson Federal Credit Union

Dillard's Federal Credit Union

Arkansas Employees Federal Credit Union

Arkansas Superior Federal Credit Union

Alcoa Community Federal Credit Union

Arkansas Federal Credit Union

Carter Federal Credit Union

Hope Credit Union

Eastman Credit Union

Employees Federal Credit Union

Morning Star Federal Credit Union

Oklahoma Central Credit Union

Tulsa Federal Credit Union

Oklahoma's Credit Union

Western Sun Federal Credit Union

Communication Federal Credit Union

State Farm Federal Credit Union

Navy Federal Credit Union

SchoolsFirst Federal Credit Union

The Golden 1 Credit Union

First Technology Federal Credit Union

Patelco Credit Union

America First Credit Union

Kinecta Federal Credit

Logix Federal Credit Union

California Credit Union

Alaska USA Federal Credit Union

Star One Credit Union

Premier America Credit Union

Los Angeles Federal Credit Union

Educational Employees Credit Union

Southland Credit Union

San Diego County Credit Union

Stanford Federal Credit Union

Redwood Credit Union

Travis Credit Union

Desert Financial Credit Union

Provident Credit Union

Reno City Employees Federal Credit Union

Pahranagat Valley Federal Credit Union

Las Vegas UP Employees Federal Credit Union

Financial Horizons Credit Union

WestStar Credit Union

Elko Federal Credit Union

Sierra Pacific Federal Credit Union

Plus Credit Union

Churchill County Federal Credit Union

Greater Nevada Credit Union

One Nevada Credit Union

Clark County Credit Union

Silver State Schools Credit Union

Boulder Dam Credit Union

Partners Federal Credit Union

Valley Strong Credit Union

NuVision Federal Credit Union

Premier America Credit Union

California Coast Credit Union

California Credit Union

Technology Credit Union

SAFE Credit Union

Chevron Federal Credit Union

Mission Federal Credit Union

TDECU Credit Union

American Airlines Federal Credit Union

Security Service Federal Credit Union

JSC Federal Credit Union

PSECU Credit Union

BECU Credit Union

Wings Financial

Ent Credit Union

DCU Credit Union

Shell Federal Credit Union

Anheuser-Busch Employees' Credit Union

Primeway Federal Credit Union

Austin Telco Federal Credit Union

Texas Trust Credit Union

Forth Worth Community Credit Union

Premier America Credit Union

Credit Human

University Federal Credit Union

Navy Army Community Credit Union

Credit Union of Texas

AMOCO Federal Credit Union

A+ Federal Credit Union

United Heritage Credit Union

Shell Federal Credit Union

Veridian Credit Union

Lake Michigan Credit Union

Bethpage Federal Credit Union

Delta Community Credit Union

Pentagon Federal Credit Union

Mountain America Credit Union

Suncoast Credit Union

GNO Federal Credit Union

Jefferson Parish Employees Federal Credit Union

WYMAR Federal Credit Union

Southwest Louisiana Credit Union

Xplore Federal Credit Union

ANECA Federal Credit Union

New Orleans Firemen's Federal Credit Union

Barksdale Federal Credit Union

Neighbors Federal Credit Union

Jefferson Financial Federal Credit Union

Campus Federal Credit Union

EFCU Financial

La Capitol Federal Credit Union

Pelican State Credit Union

Carter Federal Credit Union

CSE Federal Credit Union

OnPath Federal Credit Union

Louisiana Federal Credit Union

Baton Rouge Telco Federal Credit Union

Essential Federal Credit Union

Quachita Valley Federal Credit Union

RiverLand Credit Union

Centric Federal Credit Union

Meritus Credit Union

Bossier Federal Credit Union

Signal Financial Federal Credit Union

GSA Federal Credit Union

InFirst Federal Credit Union

Andrews Federal Credit Union

Lafayette Federal Credit Union

D.C. Teachers Federal Credit Union

Government Printing Office Federal Credit Union

IDB Global Federal Credit Union

Department of Commerce Federal Credit Union

DC Credit Union

AgFed Credit Union

United States Senate Federal Credit Union

Georgetown Federal Credit Union

Advantage Financial Federal Credit Union

HUD Federal Credit Union

Lee Federal Credit Union

Bank-Fund Staff Federal Credit Union

EP Federal Credit Union

Treasury Department Federal Credit Union

PAHO/WHO Federal Credit Union

DVA Federal Credit Union

CommonWealth One Federal Credit Union

FRB Federal Credit Union

Congressional Federal Credit Union

National Geographic Federal Credit Union

DGE Federal Credit Union

Pepco Federal Credit Union

Asbury Federal Credit Union

Spectra Credit Union

GSA Federal Credit Union

IBERIA Bank

Trustmark Bank

Pinnacle Bank

Sargent Federal Credit Union

FedChoice Federal Credit Union

US Postal Service Federal Credit Union

Justice Federal Credit Union

NIH Federal Credit Union

DGE Federal Credit Union

EP Federal Credit Union

Bfs Federal Credit Union

NLRB Federal Credit Union

OAS Staff Federal Credit Union

AFL-CIO Employees Federal Credit Union

Police Credit Union

Phi Beta Sigma Federal Credit Union

American Broadcast Employee Federal Credit Union

(TEFCU) TE Federal Credit Union

St. Gabriel's Federal Credit Union

Washington Typographic Credit Union

Transportation Federal Credit Union

Department of Labor Federal Credit Union

Eagle Bank

Congressional Bank

United States Senate Federal Credit Union

Democracy Federal Credit Union

GEICO Credit Union

Napfe Federal Credit Union

Census Federal Credit Union

Agriculture Federal Credit Union

First Horizon Bank

Howard University Federal Credit Union

Old Hickory Credit Union

US Community Credit Union

Knoxville Teachers Federal Credit Union

Bowater Employees Credit Union

Southeast Financial Credit Union

Memphis City Employees Credit Union

UT Federal Credit Union

The Tennessee Credit Union

COMTRUST Federal Credit Union

Alcoa Tenn Federal Credit Union

Heritage South Community Credit Union

First South Financial Credit Union

Enrichment Federal Credit Union

FEDEX Employees Credit Association

Leaders Credit Union

Consumer Credit Union

Eastman Credit Union

Ascend Federal Credit Union

Knoxville TVA Employees Credit Union

ORNL Federal Credit Union

Tennessee Valley Federal Credit Union

Y-12 Federal Credit Union

Home Federal Bank of Tennessee

FirstBank Holding CO

CBBC Bank

Triump Bank

Apex Bank

CIT Bank

US Bank

Fifth Third Bank

Renasant Bank

ServisFirst Bank

The Bank OF Fayette County

Franklin Synergy Bank

SunTrust Bank

Highlands Union Bank

NobleBank & Trust

SouthPoint Bank

Phenix-Girard Bank

State Bank and Trust

Merchants Bank of Alabama

Oakworth Capital Bank

EvaBank

BankFirst

Citizens Bank & Trust

Renasant Bank

Hometown Bank of Alabama

River Bank & Trust

First Community Bank of Central Alabama

Exchange Bank

Cullman Savings Bank

SunSouth Bank

FirstBank

First Southern Bank

First Citizens Bank

Progress Bank

First Federal Bank

United Bank

Traditions Bank

Southern States Bank

Farmers & Merchants Bank

CCB Community Bank

Century Bank

FNB Bank

TD Bank

Wells Fargo

Citibank

PNC

HSBC

Barclays

Bank of Baroda

State Bank of India

Axis Bank

Tata Capital

HDFC Bank

Kotak Mahindra Bank

Federal Bank

South Indian Bank

Independent Bank

Desert Financial Credit Union

OneAZ Credit Union

Arizona Federal Credit Union

Vantage West Credit Union

Hughes Federal Credit Union

TruWest Credit Union

Credit Union West

Pima Federal Credit Union

First Credit Union

SunWest Federal Credit Union

5 Things To Remember Before You Try To Get A Loan

*Assets and Liabilities

*Monthly debt payments

*Employer's contact information

*Credit score and credit history.

*Personal references

*Make sure there is no fraud alert on your credit report

Credit Bureau Contact Information

Equifax Mailing Address

Equifax Credit Information Services, LLC
P.O. Box 740241, Atlanta, GA 30374

Equifax Phone Numbers:

866-349-5186: Dispute Credit Report Items
800-685-1111: Request Free Credit Report
888-766-0008: Place Fraud Alert on Profile
866-493-9788: Existing Customer Support
888-202-4025: Business Solutions
404-885-8078: Fax Number

Experian™

Experian Mailing Address

Experian National Consumer Assistance Center
P.O. Box 4500, Allen, TX 75013

Experian Phone Numbers:

800-509-8495: Dispute Credit Report Items
888-397-3742: Report Requests & Fraud Help
877-284-7942: Existing Customer Support
888-243-6951: Business Credit Services
972-390-4908: Fax Line

TransUnion.

TransUnion Mailing Address

TransUnion Consumer Relations
P.O. Box 2000, Chester, PA 19016-2000

TransUnion Phone Numbers:

800-916-8800: Disputes Items & Status Checks
877-322-8228: Free Annual Credit Report
800-888-4213: Purchase Credit Report
888-909-8872: Place a Security Freeze
800-493-2392: Credit Monitoring Customer Support
866-922-2100: Business Services Assistance
610-546-4771: Fax Machine

Innovis

Attn: Consumer Assistance
P.O. Box 1689
Pittsburgh, PA 15230-1689
(800) 540-2505

www.innovis.com
For Innovis corporate headquarters, contact:

Innovis
250 E. Town St.
Columbus, Ohio 43215

Contact Information for PRBC Inc. (Payment Reporting Builds Credit)

A fifth credit reporting company is PRBC Inc., which performs the same functions as the other CRCs. However, it also allows consumers to build reports and a positive credit history using alternative data, such as timely bill, utility, and insurance payments. PRBC Inc. uses information not always reported to the other bureaus, allowing consumers to rebuild a positive credit history. The company is owned by MicroBilt Corporation.

MicroBilt Corporation

1640 Airport Rd, Suite 115
Kennesaw, GA 30144
(800) 884-4747
www.microbilt.com

Additional Mailing Address for credit bureaus.

TransUnion
P.O. Box 6790
Fullerton, CA 92834

Experian
P.O. Box 9530
Allen, TX 75013

Experian
P.O. Box 9532
Allen, TX. 75013

Experian
P.O. Box 4500
Allen, TX. 75013

Equifax
P.O. Box 740241
Atlanta, GA 30374

CSC Credit Services
P.O. Box 619054
Dallas, TX. 75261-9054

Telephone numbers to order your paper credit report from the three major credit bureaus.

Equifax: 1-800-685-1111
Experian: 1-888-397-3742
TransUnion: 1-800-888-4213

Addresses for three major credit bureaus fraud departments.

TransUnion
Fraud Victim Assistance Department
P.O. Box 6790
Fullerton, CA. 92634-6790

TransUnion
Fraud Department
P.O. Box 34012
Fullerton, CA. 92834

Equifax
Consumer Fraud Division
P.O. Box 740241
Atlanta, GA. 30374-0241

Equifax
Fraud Assistance
P.O. Box 105069
Atlanta, GA. 30348
1-404-885-8000
1-800-525-6285
Fax: 1-770-375-2821

Experian
National Consumer Assistance
P.O. Box 2104
Allen, TX. 75013
1-888-397-3742

Experian
P.O. Box
Allen, TX. 75013

To report the fraudulent use of your checks:

Check Rite
Phone: 800-766-2748

Chex
Systems
Phone: 800-328-5121

CrossCheck
Phone: 800 552-1900

Equifax-Telecredit
Phone: 800-437-5120

NPC
Phone: 800-526-5380

SCAN
Phone: 800-262-7771

Tele-Check
Phone: 800 366-2425

REMOVE YOUR NAME FROM PRE-APPROVED CREDIT LISTS?

Call: (888) 5OPTOUT (888-567-8688)
Removes your name from pre-approved credit lists compiled by Equifax, Experian, and Trans Union.

REMOVE YOUR NAME FROM DIRECT MAIL LISTS?

E-mail: www.the-dma.org
Write: Direct Marketing Association
Mail Preference Service
P.O. Box 643
Carmel, NY 10512

REMOVE YOUR NAME FROM TELEPHONE LISTS?

E-mail: www.the-dma.org
Write: Direct Marketing Association
Telephone Preference Service
P.O. Box 1559
Carmel, NY 10512

REMOVE YOUR NAME FROM E-MAIL LISTS?

E-mail: www.e-mps.org

Professional association of elected state attorneys general. This site provides links to each state's website, where you can find consumer protection information specific to your state.

Federal Trade Commission (FTC)
CRC 240
Washington, DC 20580
www.ftc.gov
877-382-4357

Government agency that supervises the activities of credit bureaus, repair clinics, and collection agencies.

FTC'S Identity Theft Hotline
www.consumer.gov/idtheft
1-877-IDTHEFT (1-877-438-4338)

Hotline charged with collecting complaints about identity theft at its regional offices. They also can provide an Identity Theft Affidavit that you can submit to your creditors.

Information and Education Resources

This section will provide you with agencies that provide information and education in regards to your credit as well as debt.

Consumer Information Center
Pueblo, CO 81009
www.pueblo.gsa.gov
1-800-FED-INFO (1-800-333-4636)

Federal government central distribution center for consumer information.

Membership organization that promotes ethical business practices. It provides referrals to the local office that serves the area where the company you are doing business with is located. It can help to resolve issues evolving from identity theft.

National Association of Attorneys General (NAAG)
750 First St. NE, Suite 1100
Washington, DC 20002
www.naag.org
202-326-6000

www.ingramcontent.com/pod-product-compliance
Lightning Source LLC
LaVergne TN
LVHW022102200926
848481LV00003B/1033
* 9 7 9 8 2 9 5 6 2 2 1 7 5 *